NETWORK OF ENTERPRISES AND NETWORK-ENTERPRISES

Mauro Tommaso De Candia

0. NETWORK OF ENTERPRISES OR NETWORK-ENTERPRISES?

In the last few years, within the scientific and managerial debate about enterprises and organizations, the word "network" became increasingly popular. Network of enterprises, industrial network, organizational network, business network, network-firms, are all words used with reference to traditional or new types of business and economic settings.

A large part of the literature points out that economic, technological, *inter-organizational relations* are the emerging reality of today's organizations, both the non-profit and the business ones. Links among organizations seem more explicative and predictive of performances and development than the internal structure itself of individual organizations.

Strong and weak ties are the basis of industrial networks. The thesis of this paper is that we should go on in studying the *networks of organizations* (industrial networks, industrial districts, alliances, etc.) but that we are also facing the rise of new forms of individual organizations, the *network organization*s (network firms, network public organizations). Medium and big enterprises and some public administrations tend to internally decentralize and to operate through permanent relationships with subcontractors and clients: this may give rise to a new pattern of enterprise.

Our point here is that in both cases *(network of organizations and network-organizations)* economic or information networks among big, medium and small enterprises cannot only be reduced to "flows" as business processes, information systems, logistics, and learning processes. They indeed give birth to (and are generated by) complex organizations, relying on paradigms and rules different either from the "hierarchy" (large companies) or from the pure "market" (transactions among small and medium companies).

Nature features and operative rules of those *network enterprises* have many points in common and both move away different from the traditional forms of enterprise. An emerging paradigm of organization may take place.

1. NEW FORMS OF ENTERPRISES IN ITALY

Italy - like many industrialized countries as Japan, USA, Canada, France - has been a laboratory of new relationships among enterprises in the market. This leads also to new forms of internal organization of the firms.

Different developments displaying some common features occurred in Italy in the last 10 Years.

·Large firms and medium-size companies: networks beyond flat hierarchies and increasing subcontracting and outsourcing.

Large corporations in the last couple of decades were going to flat their organizational structure. The process of creating *"short firms"* or *"flat hierarchies"* in most cases did not end up with the reduction of staff and of unnecessary management layers only. This process also generated more autonomy and responsibility to the internal organization units as divisions, business units, process centred unit, teams, roles, etc. Most corporations developed in this way a sort of "internal networks" of semi-autonomous units.

Large corporations rely more and more on outside contractors or suppliers. They do not only "buy" more than "make", but they externalize manufacturing processes and outsource services: I call them *"transactional firms*, because they get competitive advantages" displacing costs outside the firm and/or buying products and services cheaper than their internal costs. Those firms are pushed to establish further new forms of structures, policies, and operating systems aimed at affecting the organization, quality standards, and the expertise of the subcontractors, in order to improve the overall costs, quality, timeliness, and process innovation.

The relationships among the main company and the suppliers were not only based upon contracts and the economic transactions. A certain degree of intrusion in the organizational and technical affairs of the subcontractors has been usual. However, the sub-contractors, from their side, are less frequently one-client supplier: more often they are entirely "on the market," as they either work for a number of contractors or sell directly their products to the end-consumer. Subcontractors are often either large specialized firms operating based on economies of scale or small companies (giving rise to a sort of galaxy or "macro-enterprise"). Both usually operate well beyond the economic, legal and organizational control of the central corporation even though they are affected by it both economically and organizationally.

The central enterprise dealing with independent suppliers tends to integrate its internal structures and its external subcontractors less by legal rules and more though the operating systems (planning systems, information systems, logistics, reporting systems, etc.) and the "soft" management tools (corporate culture, management philosophy, corporate image, etc.). Contracting and sub-contracting firms often share them.

Partnerships and co-maker ships are the evolution on the sheer increase in the proportion of "buy and make". In addition, it is a step forwards a structural change in both the big company and subcontractors. For example in Italy the Fiat headquarter first decreased many layers in the organizational chart ending with a redundancy of thousands of employees and managers. Fiat Auto on its side subcontracts a great majority of what it is sold in a single car and further outsourcing services were done. In information services, training. However, cost reductions so achieved were not enough. Fiat was seeking a structural competitiveness given by a full co-operation of internal and of external structures in getting competitive advantages for both, consequently Fiat is moving ahead beyond the "short organization" and the "transactional firm" toward the model of a *"network firm"*, managing internal and external unit, as they were a single organization. The paradox was that for doing that, Fiat was forced to give more autonomy to subcontractors and to the internal units as well.

Another example could be given by the Italian medium enterprises, which were born or developed along the model of central agencies, which animate internal and external networks: the new "mini-multinationals" (in Italy Luxottica, Natuzzi, Riello, Valentino, SCM, etc.) are the new backbones of the Italian economy. They seem to generate maximum advantages for the company as well as for franchisee, subcontractors, and services providers.

·Non-manufacturing/ non-direct sale industries

Benetton, Stefanel, Arquati, (like Nike, or Shwinn in USA, Zara) have a "total-personnel-to-personnel-engaged-in-manufacturing" ratio below 1%. They mostly sell through a franchising system. Independent workshops and stores are located at home and in foreign countries. However, this extreme degree of externalization of operations does not change the nature of industrial companies: market and manufacturing strategy as well as key resources (financial, image, brand) are fully under control of the entrepreneur.

In those instances subcontractors and franchisees do not only operate on the market but are also a part of a "network organization" (a "super-organization") with very strong ties. The "focal organization" that is the "strategic agency", is very small in personnel and physical facilities but actually runs the "network" through few key levels: trademark, advertising, product, marketing, logistics, information network, style of stores and a few others.

·Association and co-operatives

In Italy, Confederations of Crafts, Production Co-operatives, Craftsmen Associations (like CNA) or "Rural Banks" (Casse Rurali), are networks of small and medium concern, which display *strong associative links and syndicated service structures*. An even stronger form of that is represented by the Consumers' Co-operatives case: independent companies traditionally controlling different territories but recently also in co-operation and competition among themselves at national level, which share the same trade mark, brand, purchasing consortium, warehouses. A "common flag", a common culture and a complete control of the same chain of value and visibility create the network in all of those cases in the whole system.

·*strings* and *constellations* of companies.

Systems of companies interlocked into the same business cycle are frequent in Italy. They usually have neither financial nor organizational ties and only seldom execute formal agreements between them. However, they have powerful interconnected operating systems. Examples could be indicated in the business of furniture in Brianza, of shoes in Varese, of mechanical and electronic appliances in Emilia.

·Industrial districts

Industrial districts are systems of small and medium companies operating in the same business area (textiles in Prato, furniture in Marche, shoes in Varese etc.) or in the same technology (machine tools in Piacenza or in Rimini). They include independent operating companies having the same business objective and in the same urban or regional settlements. They compete among themselves more than co-operate but they share the same pooled resources (commercial visibility of the "town-company", technological expertise, skilled workforce, subcontracting firms), and enjoy a favourable "entrepreneurial environment". These cases characterize a substantial part of Italy's economic and social structure: In the literature, they have been known such as: cases of "flexible specializations" in Emilia, "town-enterprise" like in Prato or Sassuolo, etc.

•Alliances

Agreements between companies, especially in telecommunications, electronics and chemical sectors, have only partially an economic content. These agreements design and regulate matters such as business ideas, business portfolio structures, R&D processes, for procedures, resource allocation, manufacturing systems, logistics, information systems and telecommunications, human resource development policies, etc. In a few words, an "organization" shared by different entrepreneurial subjects (a "super-organization" or a "network-organization") is in many instances generated and made visible by agreements instead of being dictated by corporate charts functions.

•Scientific Parks and Techno-polis

Highly-innovation areas, or "technology parks," like Silicon Valley, Boston Route 128, or Lyon, or the Italian Techno-polis, are an emerging form of business systems including networking and intense inter-organizational relationships and exchange of any kind of resource. Competition and co-operation coexist among universities, big companies, small companies, public administration. As a result, many of the most successful among those high-tech contexts look like a complex network organization with a single "big goal", a single flag, a single integrative mechanism rather than an aggregate of dispensed organizations served by common technological and financial resources.

• ### What do they have in common?

What do all the mentioned so different examples have in common? We have so far mentioned big, medium and small firms, network of organizations and organizations that are based on strong and weak ties, co-operation, and competition.

First, they are not merely regulated by the traditional bureaucracies, nor by pure market. They all have strategies and processes extended beyond the boundaries of the individual firms or organizations included within the network. They more precisely have in common some or most of the following features:

- main unitary processes involving all the units
- explicit or implicit recognizable inter-firm strategies
- flow of pooled and managed resources, (financial, technological and human) crossing different enterprises
- agreements and alliances among competitors
- entrepreneurial atmosphere in local regions

A different solution to the classical global/local, decentralization/centralization opposition was given by those developments.

The Italian laboratory in the business world has registered - as elsewhere - the exponential growth of something traditionally named *centralization* and *globalization:*

- mergers strongly increased in the last decade
- national and international acquisitions
- globalization and radical redefinition of business
- global mobility of capitals and technologies through international huge investments. International capital is heavily present in the Italian privatisation process of state-owned firms
- global rapid diffusion of technologies (as the 2-year lifecycle of the most innovative electronic components) require a large amount of resources for R&D in the strategic areas

The Italian laboratory has registered at the same time - more than elsewhere - the exponential growth of *localisation and decentralisation*:

- development of regional economics: Marche (Ancona), Veneto (Venice), northern Lombardy (Como) etc.
- large companies subcontracting extensively to local firms
- outsourcing of manufacturing and of services to other countries, Eastern Europe, Far East;
- co-operation among private enterprises, universities and Public Administration in local settings
- stronger links among independent companies belonging to the same "filiere" through information systems, logistics, shared market programs, telecommunications.

The coexistence of global and local, centralization versus decentralization seems a paradox. Network enterprises seem able to deal positively with this paradox. Network enterprises can be global and local at the same time, as the traditional big and small firms cannot be.

Within these concerns, radical changes affect the component subject of the described concern:

- flatting hierarchical pyramids and reducing bureaucracy in the big and medium-sized firms included in the network
- increasing autonomy of the organization units component of big-medium firms ("quasi-firms")
- high profitability, innovation and orientation to the global market of the medium-sized firms
- independence and customer orientation of the small size companies
- individual competencies and new organizational professions
- etc.

2. WHAT DOES "NETWORK ENTERPRISE" MEAN?

All of the mentioned examples illustrate the importance and the increasing variety of links among firms and institutions.

In many cases sets of individual and independent organizations developing co-operation and competition among themselves within a "global concern" or an "overall setting" which is a new paradigm of enterprise. We will name these organizations "network-organizations", "network-firms". They, just like any organization, are defined by purposive actions, goals, control on resources, boundaries, but they encompass several distinctive organizational subjects.

Most of the mentioned networked or network organizations give them advantage on traditional firms.

- They achieve results for both the individual firm and the global system (network) controlling the same value chain. This means that effectiveness and efficiency outcomes are looked for both the individual nodes and the system.
- They are the result of the continuous and purposeful design or re-design of the same business process crossing many

organizations: they do not make business process requirements they "are" BPR
- They include component organization that communicate and have concern for other organizations
- They encompass at the same time competitive and cooperative relationships among the component firms
- They develop the culture of negotiation, long-term relationship and at some extent; they seem a device for communication and negotiation.
- It is allowed that every member of a network could also be a member of other network. Some members could be a focal organization in a network, being a less important organization in the others.

In this paper, we concentrate on business organizations: network-enterprises, or network-firms, industrial networks, industrial districts: but networks become applicable in the Public Administration, in the scientific community, in the non-profit organization.

Network enterprise(s) are in fact "hybrid" enterprises between "market and hierarchies". This means that in any example provided:

- a boundary of the network could be identified and it includes at least the main processes, goals and members of the network firm. As any other firm this composite type of firm has its own strategy (a purposeful action of setting mission, general goals, expected results, value chain, etc.) and a structure (membership, division of tasks and responsibility, basic rules of behaviour, etc.).

- the control over essential system processes is kept to a minimum and it is frequent assured by a "strategic agency". Each member achieves its own goals and interests but the global system has some self-preservation mechanisms in case of danger; minimum resources are stored somewhere in the system and used in case of external challenges.

- organizations within the network not only buy or sell products and services to each other in a real free or quasi-free market. These companies are in some way an *"organized market"* which takes a large room of what traditionally was the internal organization, the internal "hierarchy". Each of these firms mould or purposively design their own organization in relation to the others and they conversely influence or co-determine the organization of others'.

- component parts of a network enterprise are first of all participant enterprises; then semi-autonomous organization units that are part of the former, and finally persons. This means an increasing weight of negotiation, strategies taking care of strategies of the others. Each component company takes the strategy of the others into account. The latter partly operate based on the "internalized market strategy" of the others. To do so, it should be developed a vision of the other's organization, which becomes increasingly the other face of the coin of *"its own strategy"*.

3. NETWORKS OF ENTERPRISES

Industrial districts, as it is well known, are systems of small and medium companies operating in the same business area (textiles in Prato, furniture in Brianza, shoes in Montebelluna etc.) or in the same technology (machine tools in Emilia-Romagna). They sometimes include independent organizations competing among themselves. More frequently, they are companies interlocked into the same business cycle: they usually have neither financial nor organizational ties and only seldom execute formal agreements between them but have powerful interconnected processes and realize "systems of flexible specialization". In all cases however they share the same common goods or pooled resources (marketing of the "town-company", technological expertise, skilled workforce, subcontracting firms, educational facilities and so on), they accumulate social capital and enjoy a common code of trust (Mutti). They grow in a favourable "entrepreneurial environment". These industrial or entrepreneurial districts have been celebrated and studied as a special feature of Italian economy (Becattini, Brusco, and Bagnasco). The positive balance between economy and society, the dance of cooperation and competition, the collective learning and the flexible specialization which characterized those districts was so influential to be seen inappropriately as a possible alternative to mass production (Piore and Sabel). The international competition put in crisis the traditional model but new models of augmented districts, large districts, and extended clusters are emerging. Those facts and researches explored the condition to develop regional economies and firms that may produce economic and social capital (Trigilia 2005).

The economists consider large and medium companies in many cases, as main contractors, the locomotives of districts (Varaldo).

I distretti in Italia							
Lombardia	15	Friuli V.G.	3	Lazio	1		
Veneto	8	Liguria	3	Abruzzo	1		
Emilia-R.	7	Sardegna	3	Molise	1		
Piemonte	7	Trentino	2	Basilicata	1		
Marche	5	Campania	2				
Toscana	4	Puglia	2				

Sole 24 Ore, 22.4.1992

	Reti centralizzate o asimmetriche	Reti paritetiche
Reti equity	Capital venture	Joint ventures
Reti non equity	Franchising, subcontracting	Consorzi
Contrattuali ad alto grado di formalizzazione	Licensing	
Contrattuali a basso grado di formalizzazione	Costellazioni	Distretti
Reti non equity non contrattuali ad alto grado di formalizzazione		Associazioni, cartelli, interlocking directorates
Reti non equity non contrattuali a basso grado di formalizzazione	Reti sociali e interpersonali	Reti sociali e interpersonali
Reti informatiche	Network, client server	Networks, client server

4. LARGE AND MEDIUM COMPANIES AS NETWORK ENTERPRISES

4.1. Converging strategies: costs, competitiveness and innovation

Within global competition, a large and medium firm pursues contradictory and converging strategies.

Firms often pursue strict <u>strategies of cost:</u> reduction of indirect labour, elimination of stocks, reduction of materials and space, as well as reduction of re-manufacturing and customer services, increase of flexibility in resource utilization, technological downsizing, etc. *(operating cheaper)*.

Besides the reduction of product/service costs, <u>competitive strategies</u> also include quicker "time to market", faster delivery and maintenance terms, quality upgrading, better visibility of the product/service offer, and of the company itself *(operating better)*.

<u>The business portfolio strategies</u> often foresee a high innovation level within products/services (not only in technology, but also in organization and in professional skills). The core service together with other engineered and personalized services.

Three-associated action are therefore required to most firms at the same time:

1. Economy of scale is still required but not necessarily through the huge castles encompassing high volume of through-put (where there is a scale of costs, not of values). Therefore:
- The "flat firm" is a step towards cost reduction
- Big or small specialized units succeed because produce (or distribute) at lower costs (flexible specialization)
- Long tail, selling products on a small bath to many people
- Internalization or externalization expand on the basis of reduction of production costs and transaction costs

2. Economy of responsiveness to market changes: segmentation is intended to meet new customer needs and to achieve a higher costumer satisfaction. This brings to the end of the primacy of the planning and marketing departments in the relations with the market. It gets more diffusion:
- Company Total Wide Quality Programs
- Customer orientation programs
- Customer oriented units

3. Economy of innovation spread innovative programs and it brings to the end the segregated "reservation of geniuses" of concentrated R&D departments.
Productivity and innovation of the research is based upon:
- Communication
- Specialisation
- Networking

Companies are asked to do all their best to survive and develop, adopting at the same time different strategies. Network enterprises can better support multiple strategies than centralized enterprises.

4.2. Structural competitiveness and structural flexibility

The idea of a *network enterprise* is founded on the following main needs of global/local economy:

• *Structural competitiveness. Competitiveness* means to be able to achieve competitive performances and keep competitive advantages getting more and more internal efficiency and value for customers. *Structural* means that this competitiveness not only comes from a contingent business-process redesign and/or strategic repositioning programs but from the intrinsic characteristics of the company shape and from the resources that it is able to mobilise permanently.

• *Network of processes.* Business processes overpass the boundaries of the traditional corporate "castle" as well as its internal functional structures. Inter-functional and intercorporate "network of processes" are the nervous system of the network-enterprise.

• *Network of people.* Processes not only exist when they are visible in procedures, technologies, expertise, but also when they are clear in "people's mind". The process is the strongest and possible "principle of reality" for people working (inside and outside the walls of the bureaucratic organization of the "castle"). Within this perspective, behaviour is not lead by being obedient to hierarchy, to rules and procedures, but by orientation in achieving measurable results (quantity, quality, costs, flexibility, and innovation).

People should understand the nature of these processes (uncertainty, degree of indeterminateness, product value, etc.) and to be able to communicate with each other in view of the results of these processes.

A network of people can only support a process in a network organization, *which* is the most important constituent part of the network enterprise.

• *Value network.* Efficacy and efficiency can be affected by:

  - optimal relationships between fixed and variable costs

- optimization of costs among internal and external resources to attain productive and service activities
- optimization of costs of co-ordination, economic distribution, communicating and obtaining information depending from different mix made of internal and external resources
- time and investment expenditures necessary to reach the "core" of business processes
- time and investment expenditures necessary to develop innovative skills

Therefore, the objective value of processes is function of the optimal combination of efforts of internal and external units performing the main business processes.

5. THE CONSTITUTIVE ELEMENTS OF NETWORK OF ENTERPRISES AND OF NETWORK ENTERPRISES

We suggest adopting the concept of network organization, both in cases of network of various enterprises and in cases of unique enterprise operating though an extensive outsourcing under two conditions

a) A network-organization exist whether it could be described and analyzed in its structure as well as in its processes: a sound descriptive and interpretative model should evaluate whether it has clear boundary, membership, goals, operating rules

b) A network-organization exist whether it is managed.

The constitutive elements of a network organization have been identified (Butera 2001) as follows.

1. There is a unique **value chain**

2. The network organization is first identified through its **main processes** crossing various component organizations. Network organizations are by nature process-centred-organizations. Economic and social value is created for component organizations and for the whole.

3. The network organization is composed by relatively self-regulated vital systems (or "**nodes**"). Firms, administrations, institutions, organizational units, roles, and individuals are vital systems selfishly engaged for their survival and growth but at the same time interacting with each other through games of cooperation and competition (Axelrod). Non-bureaucratic large corporations, small and medium flexible and innovative enterprises, service oriented administrations, business units, process centred units, teams; open roles and professions are examples of such vital nodes.

4. **Links** are another constituent part of network organizations. Strong and weak ties in an appropriate connexion often link the nodes together. This allow the nodes to interact by mutually co-operating, informing, understanding, deciding, conflicting, negotiating, performing, etc. Bureaucratic links are traditionally the most visible ones, getting the sense of an "organized system". Other types of links are however more important. Rules and practices of cooperation include working together on a problem, making a joint decision, completing a project, etc. Economic transactions include the system of costs and prices of goods and services exchanged within the system. New contractual relationships are also very important. Information through information and communication technologies are basic infrastructures of the organizations. Written, verbal and non-verbal communications are crucial links for the social processes.

5. The configuration of the whole of nodes and links gives rise to a **visible network structure**. The structures of a network organization are made up by normative structures (which

can be described and rationally designed) and by communities (based upon social regulation): Gesellschaft und Gemeinschaft (Toennies) may be no more in opposition as in the first industrial revolution. This is the result of an osmotic process between society and organizations: organizations are increasingly embedded within communities (Granovetter, Powell and Di Maggio, Bagnasco, Paci, Trigilia) and communities irrupt as relevant components of the regulation processes of the organizations (Gouldner, Butera 2004).

Examples of normative structures coexisting in a network organization are:
- Ownership structures
- Hierarchical structures (flat)
- Operating structures (process centred, a committee, a task force)
- Information structures (a local network, an ERP, a WEB platform, etc)
- Markets

Examples of communities supporting many successful networks, mainly in "regional economics" are:
- Political systems
- Family relationship
- Ethnic groups
- Organizational culture including value systems, cultures, trust, ethics, etc
- Professional systems
- Community of practices
- Clans

6. All these networks include sometimes **governance and control systems** (beyond the boundary of each individual organization) and upon larger double value chain systems (economic and social). There are also the different forms of power in the organization (Tannembaum, Locke)

7. All these networks include sometimes *sophisticate control systems upon the business processes* (beyond the boundary of each individual organization) and upon larger double value chain systems (profitability and visibility). They often have - at overall system level - business process reengineering programs, training programs, total quality programs; participation schemes; communication tools, special managerial tools (as "flag" marketing campaigns, network logistics, etc.).

6. THE PARADIGM SHIFT

Converging strategies cannot be afforded by enterprises whose culture is embedded within the traditional paradigm: a shift from "mechanistic" models of organization to "organic" models of organization, from the "castle-enterprise" to "network enterprise" is being developed in the practice of management along with developments in the management sciences.

A shift in organizational cultural paradigm is a pre-condition for the development of new models of enterprise taking place. Entrepreneurs, managers, professionals move from the *mechanistic organization* to the *organic organization* paradigm.

From the *mechanistic model of organization* made by:
- hierarchical bureaucracy
- high labour division
- men considered the spare parts
- corporate culture based upon dependency and execution

There is a move toward *organic models of organization*, including

- network of self-regulated systems
- professional roles based on minimal critical specifications
- human resources at systems components

- corporate culture based upon interaction and problem solving

A shift in the *model of enterprise* is also taking place: many enterprises move from the *"castle-enterprise"* to *"network enterprise"*. The castle enterprise is a metaphor indicating that:
- big firms were based upon economy of scale and were used to keep all resources and processes inside.
- medium firms with a 50-million-dollar sales were considered as "dwarf" companies not able to grow.
- small companies with lower technologies were usually primitive, employing cheap labour, often dependent as a detached workshops of the big firms
- research and development was usually made by great bureaucratic agencies or "reservoir of geniuses"

Network enterprises become a combination, co-operation, organized competition of identified and mobile settings:

- lean and non bureaucratic big firms
- vital medium size enterprises which have reached their right critical size for their business
- independent customer oriented small firms
- professionals employees as a building block, micro-organization units are adaptive and creative "hologram" of organizations involving a new alliance between individuals and organization
- diffused centres for science and technology in universities and firms

7. TYPOLOGY OF NETWORK ENTERPRISES

Network enterprises differ among them according to the type of control systems. We envisage a typology of four basic network enterprises:

1. Hierarchical network enterprises

They are big or medium enterprises, which go through the intense process of internal decentralization, outsourcing and subcontracting, finding out a way of making sense of the new system and let it grows, through some kind of governance. IBM, FIAT may be an example of this typology.

NETWORK OF ENTERPRISES AND NETWORK-ENTERPRISES

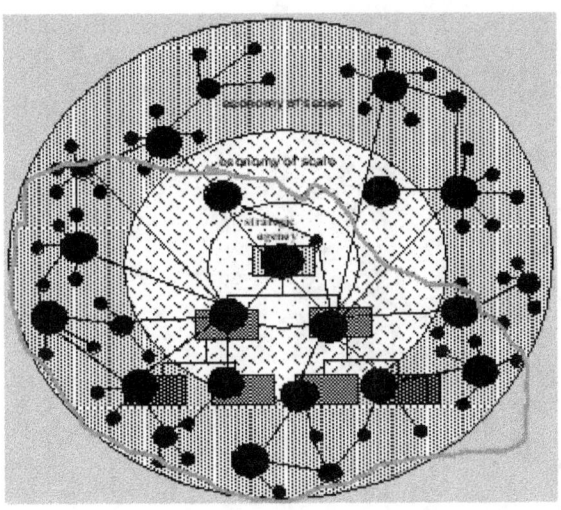

Type 1 - Hierarchical network enterprise

2. *Solar system enterprises* are cases where independent manufacturing or distribution firms turn around one strategic agency through the influence and bargaining relations (e.g., systems regulated by holding companies, "non manufacturing" industrial companies, hollow corporations, etc.). Nike, Benetton, are an example.

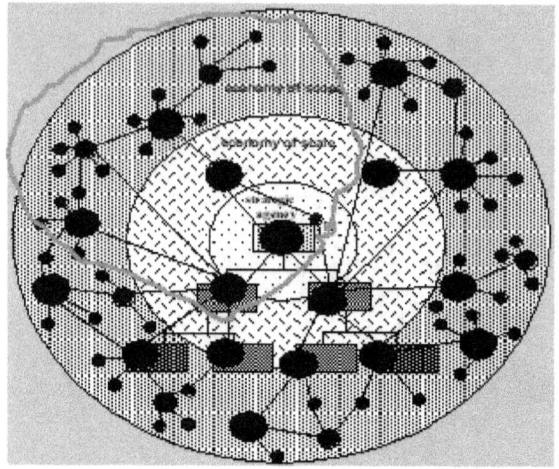

Type 2. Solar System enterprises

3. *Centreless network enterprises* (e.g., territory-based systems, industrial districts, regional systems, science parks, etc.). They should be animated instead of being managed, by collective and composite bodies including public and private organizations.

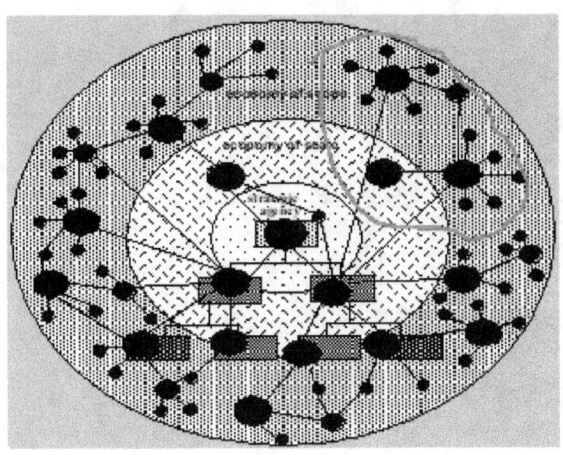

Type 3. Centreless network enterprises

4. *"Single networks enterprises"* on succeeding *"multiple gravitational centres"*, in which the system revolves around different and succeeding by important strategic agencies, with highly complex and mobile influence relations: both the major firms and the central associations attract the enterprises time by time.

In Italy, consumer co-operatives can be related to this model. They are governed - alternatively - by formal central associations or by the biggest and most profitable companies of the network.

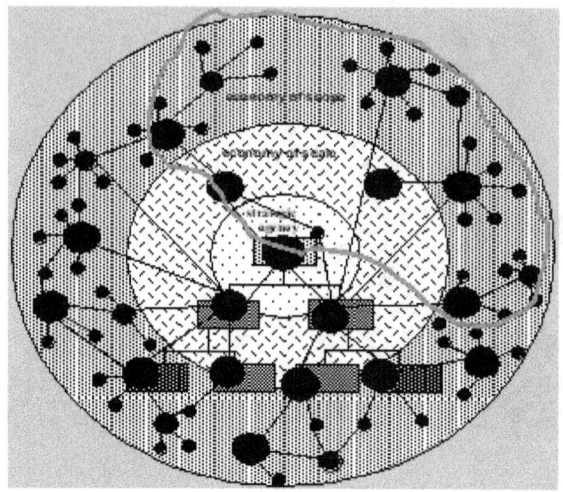

Type 4. Single network

8. IMPLICATIONS: THE ENTREPRENEUR / MANAGER'S ACTIONS

The managers and entrepreneurs of individual firms in the future should be able to manage and sometimes radically generate new business structures. Their ability to choose between market and structure, making or buying, and use both hard or soft co-ordination tools and technologies, will be a crucial issue. But more crucial will the bringing into a stylistic unity of government" a great variety of dispersed elements.

The network of enterprise require a sort of "meta-management of the strategic agency" (Butera, Alberti).

In all cases, there are *four fundamental set of actions* or "area of strategic management" for the managers and entrepreneurs working in enterprises, which - regardless of their legal status or size - are undergoing a deep structural change into more flexible patterns and/or becoming more and more strongly market-oriented.

1. *To know how to give life to (and to maintain) vital organizational nodes*

Strategic management means to give life (to select, to shape) to units that are consistent (in terms of technology, organization, and people) and adequate (to product/markets). It also means to maintain, that has to say to provide such units with adequate operational, management, and innovation skills, self-regulation abilities (how to handle commitments, communication, etc.), and the ability to achieve goals (variance control, feedback, and feed-forward). Therefore, managing systems deal with setting and controlling goals, training, supporting, and sanctioning also with closing down inefficient or ineffective units while effectively tapping experiences and preserving people. In a word, manager and entrepreneurs will be *"coacher"*.

2. To know how to interact and operate with links

Managers and entrepreneurs in the networks will not develop bureaucratic rules - but try to define *"minimum critical specifications"* that is to under-procedure. He or she will build internal markets communicating with external markets by treating both internal and external customers in the same ways. He or she will be able to develop and enhance the information technology to support professionals, along with communication and co-operation technologies. He or she will develop interdependence and problem-solving technologies and secure the development of income and visibility value chains. In a word, manager and entrepreneurs will be *"connecting agencies"*.

3. To know how to design and manage complex structures

The ability to design and manage new systemic structures (business units, profit centres, divisions, departments, workteams, technology cells, etc.) are part of the design and strategic management responsibility. The ability to manage market organizational dimensions and economic organizational dimensions is required. Developing and managing local networks; geographical networks, co-operation technologies, intelligent workstations, and DSS will increasingly become a co-operative effort of entrepreneurs and managers with computer specialists, etc.

Managing will increasingly imply the ability to manage "small human societies". Being a manager will increasingly imply taking deliberate actions to develop a corporate culture and the management of symbolic resources. In a word, manager and entrepreneurs will be "*architects*".

4. Master processes

Business process reengineering and operative process optimization will held a key role. There will be an increasing tendency to develop ad-hoc plans and control systems of the entire local processes. The enterprise language will have to be commanded as masterly as ever, but a local "house culture" should be developed as well. Incentives will have to be linked with the business management control-system. Training should be increased by amount and quality. There will be a tendency to develop systems "open roles" than jobs positions. There will be a tendency to build pathways of "*cosmopolitan professions*".

9. DESIGNING NETWORK ENTERPRISES

Is it possible to design network enterprises? We are inclined to a positive answer to the condition of identifying and designing five fundamental dimensions, which are suitable to goals/results, resources, and to power structures. They are as follows:

A. The organizational mission and the strategic goal setting.

B. The visibility of the network
Conceptual and pictorial representation should be provided of processes, nodes, links, and general outcomes.

C. The government of the network

Coalition/Co-operation should be developed together
Democratic leadership should be developed: the "prince" could be a Committee instead of an individual.
Mobile leadership should be developed: the "prince" should not be the king's son who seats on his father's throne, but rather the barbarian Teodorico who makes of the county of Raven the second Roman Empire.

D. Policies for the network enterprise nodes

Key policy issues are:
- Self-regulated units (as business units, process units, teams) within the large firms
- Medium companies modernization and consolidation
- Increasing number and quality of small companies
- Development of a work force able to act with both professional consultants and micro-entrepreneurs

E. Investments should be concentrated:
- in appropriate I.T.
- in physical local infrastructures for corporations: transportation, meeting facilities
- in cultural infrastructures such as language, social programs
- in a professionally qualified education

BIBLIOGRAPHY

Aldrich H., (1979), *Organizations and environment*, Prentice Hall, Englewood Cliffs

Aldrich H., (1972), *The Origins and Persistence of Social Networks. Social Structure and Network Analyses*, Sage, Beverly Hills, CA

Aiken M., Hage I., (1968), "Organizational Interdependence, and Intraorganizational Structure", *American Sociological Review*, n. 33

Anchordoguy M., (1990), "A Brief History of Japan Keiretsu", *Harvard Business Review*, n. 4

Antonelli C., (1988), (eds.), *New Information Technology and Industrial Change: the Italian Case*, Kluver Academic Publisher, Dordrecht

Antonelli C., (1987), "L'impresa rete: cambiamento tecnologico internazionalizzazione e appropriazione di quasi rendite", *Annali di storia dell'impresa*, n. 3

Axelrod R. M., (1984), *The Evolution of Cooperation*, Basic Books, New York, (in it., Giochi di cooperazione, Adelphi)

Axelsson B., Easton G., (1991), *Industrial Networks, A new of reality*, Routledge, London, New York

Bagnasco A., (1977), *Tre Italie*, Il Mulino, Bologna

Bagnasco A., (1986), "La costruzione sociale del mercato: strategie di impresa e esperimenti di scala in Italia", *Stato e Mercato*, n. 13

Barff R.A., (1987), "Industrial Clustering and the Organization of Production - A Point Pattern-Analysis of Manufacturing in Cincinnati", *Annals of the Association of American Geographers*, n. 1

Barley S. R., (1990), "The Alignment of Technology and Structure through Roles and Networks", *Administrative Science Quarterly*, n. 61

Barnard C. C., (1938), *The functions of the Executive*, Harvard University Press, Cambridge, MA

Barney J. B., Ouchi W. G., (1986), *Organizational Economics*, Jossey Bass,

San Francisco, CA

Becattini G., (1979), "Dal settore industriale al distretto industriale", *Rivista di Economia e Politica Industriale*, n. 1

Bellon B., Chevalier J. M., (1984), *L'Industrie en France*, Flammarion, Paris

Bengt J., (1987), "Beyond Process and Structure: Social Exchange Networks", *International Studies of Management & Organization*, n. 1

Benson J. K., (1975), "The Interorganizational Network as a Political Economy", *Administrative Science Quartetly*, n. 20

Bergman E. M., Maier G., Todtling F., (1991), *Regions Reconsidered: Economic Innovation, and Local Development in Industrialized Countries*, Mansell, London, New York

Bertelé U., Mariotti S., (eds.), (1991), *Impresa e Competizione Dinamica*, Etas Libri, Milano

Brusco S., (1982), "The Emilian model: productive decentralisation and social integration", *Cambridge Journal of Economics*, n. 6

Brusco S., (1990), *Piccole imprese e distretti industriali*, Rosenberg e Sellier, Torino

Burack E. H., Negandhi A. R., (1977), *Organization design: theoretical perspectives and empirical findings*, Kent State University Press, Kent, Ohio

Butera F., (1990), *Il castello e la rete*, Franco Angeli, Milano, (in French, (1990), *La métamorphose de l'organization*, Les Editions d'Organization, Paris)

Butera F. (2000) *Il campanile e la rete*, Il sole 24 ore

Chandler A. D., (1990), *Scale and Scope: the Dynamics of Industrial Capitalism*, Harvard Business Press, Cambridge, MA

Ciborra C., (1983), "Markets Burocracies and Groups in the information society", *Information Economics and Policy*, n. 1

Chiesi A. M., (1981), "L'analisi dei reticoli sociali: teoria e metodi", *Rassegna Italiana di Sociologia*, n. 2

Coase R. H., (1937), "The nature of the firm", *Economica New Series*, n. 4

Contractor F. J., Lorange P., (1988), "Competition vs. cooperation: a benefit/cost framework for choosing fully-owned investments and cooperative relationships", *Management International Review*, Special Issue 1988

Cook K. S., (1981), *Network Structure from Ewchange Perspectives in Social Structure and Network Analyses*, Sage, Beverly Hills, CA

Cook K. S., Emerson R., (1984), "Exchange Networks and the Analysis of Complex Organizations", *Research in the Sociology of Organizations*, JAI Press, Greenwich, Conn.

Di Maggio P., (1986), "Structural Analysis of Organizational Fields", *Research in Organizational Behaviour*, JAI Press, Greenwich, Conn.

Di Maggio P. J., Powell W. W., 1983), "The iron cage revisited", *American Sociological review*, n. 48

Dioguardi G., (1982), "Macrofirm: Construction firms for the computer age", *Journal of Construction Engineering and Management*, ASCE, Milano

Dioguardi, G., (1986), *L'impresa nell'era del computer*, Edizioni Sole 24 Ore, Milano

Dioguardi, G., (1993), "Futuro a rete per rifare l'Italia", *Mondo Economico*, July 3

Dioguardi, G., (1994), *Sistemi di Imprese*, Etas Libri, Milano

Dollinger M. J., (1990), "The evolution of Collective Strategies in Fragmented Industries", *Academy of Management Review*, n. 15

Dore R. P., (1986), *Structural adjustment in Japan, 1970-82*, ILO, Geneva

Dosi G., Orsenigo L., (1988), "Coordination and transformation: an overview of Structures, Behaviours and Change in Evolutionary Environments", paper presented at the International Workshop *"L'impresa rete"*, June, Istituto RSO, Camogli

Easton G., (1990), "Relationships Among Competitors", in Day G., Weitz B., Wensley R., *The Interface of Marketing and Strategy*, JAI Press, Greenwich, Conn.

Eccles R., Nohria N., (1992), *Networks and organizations*, Harvard University Press, Cambridge, MA

Emerson R. M., (1972), "Exchange Theory, Part II: Exchange Relations in Neworks", in Berger J., Zedditch and Andersson B., (eds), *Sociological Theories in Progress*, Houghton Mifflin, Boston, MA

Emerson R. M., (1972), "Power-dependence relations", *American Sociological Review*, n. 27

Emery F., Trist E., (1965), "The causal texture of organization", *Human Relations*, February

Evan W. M., (1966), "The Organization-Set: Toward a Theory of Interorganizational Relation", in J. Thopmson (ed.), *Approaches to Organizational Design*, University of Pittsburgh Press, Pittsburgh, PA

Evan W. M., (1976), *Interorganizational Relations*, Penguin, Harmondsworth

Gage W., Mandell M. P., (1990), *Strategies for managing intergovernmental policies and networks*, Praeger, New York

Galaskiewicz J., (1979), *Exchange Networks and Community Politics*, Sage, Beverly Hills, CA

Gillespie D. F., (1992), *Industrial networks: a new view of reality*, Routledge, London, New York

Grabher G., (1993), *The embedded firm: on the socioeconomics of industrial networks*, Routledge, London, New York

Granovetter M., (1985), "Economic action and social structure: the problem of embeddedness", *American Journal of Sociology*, n. 91

Hakansson H., (1989), *Corporate Technological Behaviour. Cooperation and Networks*, Routledge, London, New York

Hakanssoh H., (1987), *Industrial Technological Development: a Network Approach*, Croom Helm, London

Hamilton G. G., Suzuki M., (1989), "Patterns of Interfirm Control in Japanese Business", *Organization Studies*, n. 4

Hannan M. T., Freeman G., (1989), *Organizational ecology*, Harvard University Press, Cambridge, (in Italian, *Ecologia organizzativa*, Etaslibri, Milano)

Hasting C., (1993), *The new organization: growing the culture of organizational networking*, London, New York, McGraw-Hill

Hirschman, A. O., (1979), *Exit, Voice and Loyalty*, Harvard University Press, Cambridge, MA

Hodgson G., (1988), *Economics and Institutions*, Polity Press, Cambridge, UK

Hoffman A. N., Stearns T. M., Shrader C. B., (1990), "Structure, Context, and Centrality in Interorganizational Networks", *Journal of Business Research*, n. 4

Hogberg B., (1977), *Interfirm cooperation and strategic development*, BAS, Goteborg

Imai K., Itami H., (1984), "Interpretation of Organization and market.

Japan's Firms and Market in comparison with USA", *International Journal of Industrial Organization*, n. 2

Imai K., (1988), "The evolution of Japan's Corporate and Industrial Network", paper presented at the International Workshop *L'impresa rete,* Istituto RSO, Camogli, June

Jacobsen L., Illeris S., (1990), *Networks and regional development*, NordREFO, Copenhagen

Johanson J., Mattsson L. G., (1987), "Interorganizational Relations in Industrial Systems: A Network Approach Compared with the Transaction-Cost Approach", *International Studies of Management & Organization*, n. 1

Judkins P., West D., Drew J., (1989), "Networking in Organizations - The Rank Xerox Experiment", *Organization Studies*, n. 2

Levine S., White P., (1962), "Exchange as a Conceptual Framework for the Study of Interorganizational Networks", *Administrative Science Quartetly*, n. 6

Litwak E., Hylton L., (1962), "Interorganizational Analysis: A Hypothesis on Coordinating Agencied", *Administrative Science Quartetly*, n. 6

Lomi A., (1991), *Reti organizzative*, Il Mulino, Bologna

Lorenzoni G., (1992), *Accordi, reti e vantaggio competitivo*, Etas Libri, Milano

Lorenzoni G., (1985), "Dalla singola impresa agli aggregati di imprese: la costellazione", in V. Balloni, *Esperienze di ristrutturazione industriale*, Il Mulino, Bologna

Lundgren A., (1991), "Technological innovation and industrial evolution, the emergence of industrial networks", *Economic Research Institute*, Stockholm School of Economics

Magatti M., (1991), *Azione Economica come azione sociale*, F. Angeli, Milano

Mandell M. P., (1988), "Intergovernmental Management in Interoganizational Networks - A Revised Perspective", *International Journal of Public Administration*, n. 4

Meyer J., Rowan B., (1977), "Institutionalized organizations", *American Journal of Sociology*, n. 83

Nakatani I., (1984), "The economic role of financial corporate grouping", in Aoki M., (ed.),*The economic analysis of the Japanese firm*,

Elsevier, Amsterdam

Neghandi A. R. (ed.), (1975), *Interorganization Theory*, Kent State University Press, Kent, OH

Nelson R., Winter S., (1982), *An evolutionary Theory of Economic Change*, Harvard University Press, Cambridge, MA

Nishiguchi T., (1994), *Strategic industrial sourcing: the Japanese advantage*, Oxford University Press, New York

Nohria N., (1991), "The MNC as a differentiated network", *Division of Research*, Harvard Business School, Boston, MA

Nozick R., (1994), "Invisible-Hand Explanations", *The American Economic Review*, January 3-5

Nystrom P., Starbuck W. (eds.), (1981), *Handbook of Organizational Design*, Oxford University Press, New York

Ohmae K., (1989), "The global logic of strategic alliances", *Harvard Business Review*, n. 2

Orru M., Hamilton G. G., Suzuki M., (1989), "Patterns of Interfirm Control in Japanese Business", *Organization Studies*, n. 4

Peils A., et al., (1990), "Can a Keiretsu Work in America?", *Harvard Business Review*, n. 5

Perulli P., (1992), *Atlante metropolitano*, Il Mulino, Bologna

Pichierri A., (1986), *Strategie contro il declino in aree di antica industrializzazione*, Rosenberg&Sellier, Torino

Pfeffer J., Novak P. (1974), *The external control of Organizations: a Resource Dependance Model*, Harper and Row, New York

Pfeffer J., Salancik J., (1978), *The external control of organizations*, Harper and Row, New York

Piore M., Sabel C. F., (1984), *The Second Industrial Divide*, Basic Books, New York, (in Italian, *Le due vie allo sviluppo industriale*, Isedi, Torino)

Porter M., (1980), *Competitive strategy: techniques for analyzing industries and competitors*, The Free Press, New York

Powell W. W., (1990), "Neither Market nor Hierarchy - Network forms of Organization", *Research in Organizational Behavior*, n. 12

Pyke F., Becattini G., Sengenberger, (eds.), (1990), *Industrial Districts and Inter-Firm Cooperation in Italy*, International Institute for Labour Studies, Geneva

Rogers D. L., Whetten D. A., et al., (1982), *Interorganizational Coordination: Theory, Research and Implementation*, Iowa State University Press, Ames, Iowa

Romme A. G. L., (1990), "Vertical Integration as Organizational Strategy Formation Source", *Organization studies*, n. 2

Rowe F., Veltz P., (1991), *Entreprises et territoires en reseaux*, Presse de Pont et Chaussés

Rumelt R. P., (1982), "Diversification Strategy and Profitability", *Strategic Management Journal*, n. 3

Saxenian A. L., (1989), "The origins and dynamics of production networks in Silicon Valley", Institute of Urban and Regional Development, April, University of California at Berkeley, Berkeley, CA

Sabel C. F., (1988), *The reemergence of Regional Economies*, paper presented at the Conference: *L'impresa Rete*, Istituto RSO, June, Camogli

Sabel C. F., (1989), "Flexible specialization and the re-emergence of regional economies", in Hirst P., and Zeitlin J., (eds.), *Reversing Industrial Decline*, Oxford, Berg.

Scott. J., (1979), *Corporations, classes and capitalism*, St. Martin, New York

Sekkat K., (1988), "Strategic Aspects of the Concept Filières-de-Production and Its Usefulness in Industrial-Economics Source", *Cahiers économiques de Bruxelles*, n. 118

Shimokawa K., (1985), "Japan's keiretsu system", *Japanese Economic Studies*, n. 12

Signorelli A., (1992), *Relazioni interorganizzative*, Franco Angeli, Milano

Stigler G. J., Boulding K. E., (1952), *Reading in Price Theories*, R. D. Irwin, Chicago

Stinchcombe A. L., (1965), "Social structure and organizations", March J. G., (ed.), *Handbook of Organizations*, Rand McNally, Chicago

Thorelli H. B., (1986), "Networks- Between Markets and Hierarchies", *Strategic Management Journal*, n. 1

Tichy N., Fombrun C., (1979), "Network Analysis in Organizational Settings", *Human Relations*, n. 32

Vaccà S., (1993),"Grande impresa e concorrenza: tra passato e futuro", Proceedings Convegno *Economia Politica Industriale 1973-93*, November 1993, Milano, (in press, *Economia e Politica Industriale*)

Varaldo R., (1979), (ed.), *Ristrutturazione industriale e rapporti fra imprese,* F. Angeli, Milano

Weick K. E., (1969), The Social Psychology of Organization, Addison-Welsey, Reading, MA, (in Italian, Organizzare, ISEDI, Torino)

White H. C., (1981), "Where Do Market Come From?", *American Journal of Sociology,* n. 3

Williamson O. E., (1975), *Market and Hierarchies,* The Free Press, Cambridge

Williamson O. E., (1975), *Market and Hierarchies: Analysis and Antitrust Implications,* Free Press Macmillan, New York

Williamson O. E., (1981), "The modern Corporation: Origins, Evolution, Attributes", *Journal of Economic Literature,* December

Williamson O. E., (1985), *The Economic Institutions of Capitalism,* The Free Press, New York

Williamson O.E., (1987), "The logic of the firm", paper prepared for the Conference: *The nature of the Firm: Fiftieth Anniversary Celebration,* May 14-16, Yale University

Williamson O.E., (1994), "Visible and Invisible Governance", *The American Economic Review,* January 3-5

Wiewel A., Hunter A., (1985), "The Interorganizational Network As a Resource: A Comparative Case Study on Organizational Genesis", *Administrative Science Quarterly,* n. 30

Zan S., (1984), "L'analisi interorganizzativa per lo studio delle politiche pubbliche", *Rivista Trimestrale Scienze dell'Amministrazione,* n. 4

Zucker L. G., (1983), "Organizations as institutions", *Research in the Sociology of Organizations,* n. 2

www.ingramcontent.com/pod-product-compliance
Lightning Source LLC
Chambersburg PA
CBHW072237230526
45466CB00024B/2097